CONTENTS

Seven Sins of Jonah

WILLIAM
STEUART
McBIRNIE Ph.D.

Tyndale House
Publishers, Inc.
Wheaton, Illinois

Library of Congress Catalog Card Number 80-53789.
ISBN 0-8423-5876-5, paper. Copyright © 1981 by William Steuart McBirnie. First printing, March 1981. Printed in the United States of America

Some years ago, archeologists excavated a
small section of the ancient city of
Nineveh. They found in the ruins of the
royal palace a black stone obelisk on which
an ancient king of Assyria had carved a
record of his bloody conquests. The stone
is a permanent record containing a list of
the nations and famous kings conquered by
this King Shalamanezer in his military
campaign in the winter of 842 B.C. Among
others listed appears the name of Jehu, king
of Israel, a startling reference to the man
described at length in the Bible.

The terrible treatment accorded those
who opposed the Assyrians is portrayed for

us both in picture and writing discovered
by archeologists in the ruins of Nineveh.
Concerning Nineveh, Professor Maspero
writes:

> As long as a town resisted the
> besieging Assyrians, all its inhabitants
> bearing arms who fell into their hands
> were subjected to the most cruel tortures;
> they were cut to pieces, or impaled alive
> on stakes just in front of the lines so the
> besieged should enjoy a full view of the
> sufferings of their comrades. Even during
> the course of a short siege this line of
> stakes would be prolonged till it formed
> a bloody fence between the two armies.
> When a town surrendered many people
> were thrown from the tops of the towers,
> or their ears and noses cut off, or their
> hands and feet amputated, or they and
> their children were roasted over a slow
> fire, or skinned alive, or decapitated and
> their heads piled in great pyramids.

King Ashurnasirpal II of Assyria (884-859
B.C.) boasted:

> I constructed a pillar at the gate of the
> city. Then I skinned the chief men and
> covered the post with their skins and
> suspended their bodies from this same

pillar. Others I impaled on the summit of the pillar and I ranged others on stakes around the pillar.

While the memory of this Assyrian conquest was still strong in the minds of Israel, there was born in the little village of Gath-hepher in northern Palestine, of the family of Amittai, a son whom they named Jonah. The lad grew up with the tales of the ferocity of the Assyrians ringing in his ears.

In 805 B.C., while Jonah was still a boy or a young man, a new king of Assyria, Adad-Nirari, set out to again bring Israel under tribute. He recorded:

I conquered the lands of the Hittite, Amurru entirely, Tyre, Sidon, the land of Omri (Israel is called "land of Omri" after the great King Omri who ruled Israel in a previous generation).

We may be sure that Jonah saw this conquest and its horrors for himself and formed a deep hatred for the Assyrians.

When Jonah became a man, he was commissioned by God to be the Lord's prophet to Israel. He very likely attached himself to the royal court of King Jeroboam II who reigned from 790 to 749 B.C. There

is no doubt that Jonah was a faithful
herald of God's Word to the king and was
intensely patriotic.

It was this prophet, who loved his
country and hated its enemies with such
passion, whom God one day asked to go
to the capital city of the Assyrians and
preach to them God's coming judgment
on their evil deeds. The Book of Jonah is
the record of how this good prophet tried
to escape this responsibility and what
God had to do to make him willing to
bear God's message to the pagan Assyrians.
The story of Jonah has an intensely
personal message for us today. We can see
ourselves in him and profit much from
what we see.

ONE

Why the Book of Jonah Was Written

The Book of Jonah was probably not written until after Israel had been destroyed and the nation Judah's seventy-year captivity in Babylon ended and they returned to rebuild the ruined country. The only good thing which had come out of the Babylonian captivity was a deep determination by the people to preserve the wonderful revelation which God had given through Moses and the prophets to Israel and Israel alone.

It was a wonderful truth for a little people, ground under the tyranny of a great nation, to believe themselves the only possessors of the true religion. This conviction might make them an earnest missionary people, anxious to give the truth to their conquerors, or it might make them fiercely bigoted, despising their heathen conquerors whom they could not defeat. As a matter of fact, the latter was the more common feeling of many Jews in the fifth century before Christ, when the Book of Jonah was written.

The earnest effort of the great spirits of Judaism had been directed toward leading the people to a pure faith. They had found it necessary to warn the people against such alliances with other peoples as should cause them to fall away from their allegiance to Jehovah. But this had the unfortunate result that the Jew became separated, exclusive, delighting in the notion that he was the favorite of heaven, and hoping that God would mete out judgment upon his enemies. The Jew of Jonah's day did not desire that the peoples of the earth should be saved. Rather, he looked for a grand vengeance that should pay back the tyrannies that the brutal heathen had exercised upon Israel. Clearly, such a hope of vengeance did not belong to true religion.

There arose a prophet with the Spirit of God in his heart, who realized that his people were being led astray. His belief in Jehovah, and in the glory of serving him, led him to desire greatly that all men might serve him. How should he bring such a message to his people? He decided to tell them Jonah's story, the tale of a typical religious bigot, so that in reading it Israel might see itself. The Book of Jonah is a sermon story written to expose the depths of sin in an otherwise religious man.

When the Word of the Lord came to Jonah saying, "Arise, go to Nineveh," Jonah was profoundly shocked. He understood all too clearly that God's command "cry against the city" was a message not entirely of doom but possibly of repentance and forgiveness. That God could forgive the vile Assyrians was unthinkable! No! Good Jew that he was, he would have no part in any mercy for his nation's hated enemies. In a rage, he departed to Joppa, which was then, as now, a Palestinian seaport.

Jonah found a Phoenician ship bound for
Tarshish, a port in Spain, as far away from
Nineveh as he could go. He paid his fare
and, while the ship was awaiting fair winds
and the tide, he went down into the hold of
the ship and fell asleep.

The ship had barely sailed out of sight
of land when a great storm broke and
threatened the tiny vessel. The sailors
sensed the storm to be of more than normal
significance. There was a supernatural
portent about it, as if God were angry.

Jonah was awakened and, realizing he
could not run from God, confessed his

rebellion and asked the sailors to throw him overboard. The pagan sailors prayed to Jehovah and, as the Hebrew word graphically describes it, "dug the sea" with their oars in a desperate attempt to pull out of the storm without throwing Jonah into the water, but to no avail. So Jonah was heaved overboard and soon fell into the open jaws of a great sea monster that Jehovah had prepared.

The story of Jonah is full of the miraculous. The storm was a supernatural storm, the sea monster was a divinely appointed vessel. It is at this point that many have felt that the narrative departs from history and becomes fiction.

Jonah, instead of dying as he fully expected, found himself alive, if uncomfortable, in the belly of the fish. As he waited out the long hours with, as he says, "the seaweed wrapped about him," he meditated. He must have been a man of iron will, for it took three days of this dark terror before he was willing to do God's will. After he indicated he was finally willing to obey, God forced the fish to disgorge him at the shore and he went on his way, badly shaken, to Nineveh.

Nineveh, the capital city of Assyria, lay about four hundred miles to the east of Palestine. It was composed of both a rural and an urban area. The actual town itself was about three miles long and one-and-a-half miles wide. The *Westminster Bible Atlas* says, "The King's Palace was a tremendous structure. Excavators have cleared seventy-one halls lined with stone reliefs, nearly two miles in total length."

Nineveh, however, had also a large rural district within its outer walls. This huge area included this settlement of Caleb, twenty miles south of urban Nineveh, and Khorsabad, some ten miles north. Tightly packed farms and homes made this "city" of Nineveh, indeed, a wonder of the world.

The narrative says that Jonah entered into what was described as "an exceedingly great city of three days journey" from one side to another (3:3). Probably it was at least thirty miles across.

Undoubtedly, Jonah encountered Hebrew captives and slaves. They were there in abundance, according to the inscriptions found by archeologists.

Jonah began to preach. All we have of his sermon is the text, "Yet forty days and Nineveh shall be destroyed" (3:4). Whether he repeated this many times, whether he pronounced it once, or whether he elaborated on it and preached a long sermon, no one knows. In any case, the effect of the sermon was unexpected. A wave of repen-

tance rolled across the city! It entered the
palace and included the people, small and
great. It even reached to the animals in
that their owners were required by King
Adad-Nirari to decorate the beasts of
burden with the symbols of repentance and
sorrow. The king said, "Who can tell if God
will turn and repent, and turn away from
his fierce anger, that we perish not?" (3:9).

How can we explain such an astounding
sight as that of a pagan world capital in
sackcloth and ashes because of the word of
a miserable and reluctant prophet of a
conquered nation?

Perhaps the story of Jonah's miraculous
escape from the sea monster had preceded
his coming. It may or may not be a
coincidence that the word *Nineveh* comes
from a word, "NINUA," that is akin to
"NUNU" which means "fish." The very
appearance of the name *Nineveh* in the
cuneiform (wedge writing) of Assyria is the
shape of a fish in a box or tank.

The explanation of the repentance of the
people of Nineveh perhaps lies in the utter
sincerity of Jonah's speech and the striking
appearance of a man so lately escaped from
death, perhaps even blanched white by the
stomach acids from the fish. In any case,
the Ninevites repented and that allowed

God to grant them mercy and reprieve from his certain judgment.

This was not to Jonah's liking, for it meant that his nation's great enemy was to escape destruction. So, he remonstrated with God: "Is this not what I said when I was still at home? That is why I was so quick to flee to Tarshish. I knew that you were a gracious and compassionate God, slow to anger and abounding in love, a God who relents from sending calamity. Now, O Lord, take away my life, for it is better for me to die than to live" (4:2, 3, NIV). Jonah seemed to have a tendency to seek death. Three times he asked God to let him die.

Still wondering if God would not be won over to destroying these hated pagans, Jonah went outside the city and sat down to watch under a temporary booth he had made of branches. During the night, God caused a gourd to grow and, when the morning sun arose, it provided shade for the prophet who sat under a blazing sun with the temperature of his emotions almost as hot as the sun. The next night, a worm destroyed the gourd, and Jonah's compassion was touched. "Poor little gourd. Never harmed a thing, only did good. And now—dead." Then came the voice of Jehovah, "Jonah, are you sorry for the gourd and yet not sorry for the great city of Nineveh when there are more than 120,000 children not old enough to tell the difference between right and wrong?"

And here, abruptly, the story ends with no further word of what happened to Nineveh, or Jonah, or anything else. We are left only with God's declaration of compassion for all people ringing in our ears; that, of course, is enough.

THREE

Historicity of the Book

Several interesting items in this book help open it for our understanding. The first is the perennial argument as to whether the book is pure fiction or both fiction and fact. It must be noted that in the Scriptures there are many parables and hypothetical stories which tell a story to prove or illustrate a moral. It must be admitted that the argument for the story of Jonah being a parable or moral fiction cannot be lightly ignored.

As has often been stated , "The Bible is a library of various types of writing: history, poetry, philosophy, sermon, and prophecy." What more natural thing than a library including some fiction to point up a moral? But, even if it is not a disservice to believe the book of Jonah to be fiction, there is strong evidence in favor if its historicity.

Some would say, "The storm could not have been from God for God does not interfere with nature." Yet, Jesus Christ stilled the storm on Galilee! Others object, "How could anyone survive in a fish for three days and three nights?" We admit that it would have to be a miracle. But, there is nothing wrong with a miracle! After all, this is a story about God intervening in men's affairs.

Dr. Harry Rimmer told of a man living in England who fell overboard in the Mediterranean during a fishing voyage and was swallowed by a huge forty-foot fish. He was later rescued alive when the fish was caught. The man was in the fish's stomach for seventeen hours. The only effect upon him was that he was bleached by the acid in the stomach of the fish.

Then there are those who object that secular history does not record the repentance that took place at Nineveh. To this we answer that the ruins of Nineveh proper have not yet been completely excavated. A village is situated there and, while much excavation has been done in the rural area of ancient Nineveh in the palaces of

several of her kings, all the records of King
Adad-Nirari have not yet been discovered.
Only his name engraved upon his curved
sword and a few tablets have come to light.
Many gaps in Assyrian history still remain
to be filled.

Akin to the above objection is one which
expresses the doubt that a minor Hebrew
prophet could cause such a turmoil in such
a huge sophisticated metropolis as Nineveh.
To this, we say that great cities have often
been upset by less than the prophet Jonah.
Here, again, if we believe God was in this
event, we have no trouble agreeing that
God could, at his discretion, provide a stage
setting for revival.

Some assert that there is no fish capable
of sustaining a whole man inside itself.
Again, we answer "miracle" but add that
there are said to be many varieties of both
whale and shark that are quite large
enough to contain a man. Sharks of forty
feet in length have been found in the
Mediterranean.

It is in this connection that some claim
to find a contradiction between the Bible
and natural science. In the Book of Jonah,
the sea monster is called a "fish" and in the
New Testament, Jesus is quoted as calling
it a "whale." Since a whale is a mammal and
not a fish, those who could better spend

their time in less idle speculation are said to find a discrepancy. Actually, it was the King James Version translators who interpreted the word Christ used as "whale." Christ used a term meaning "sea monster" in the original language and in both the Book of Jonah and in the New Testament the kind of sea monster is not stated.

The Book of Jonah makes sound historical sense if one accepts the miraculous and supernatural as possible. If one rejects the miraculous, then neither the Book of Jonah nor the rest of the Bible is tenable.

There are facts on the positive side of the question of the historicity of Jonah. First, Jonah was a historical character according to other Scriptures:

He [Jeroboam II] restored the coast of Israel from the entering of Hamath unto the sea of the plain according to the word of the Lord God of Israel which he spake by the hand of his servant, Jonah, the son of Amittai, the prophet, which was of Gath-hepher [2 Kings 14:25].

Jonah is also characterized as an actual man. He was described as going to Joppa, an actual city, and he bought passage to Tarshish, another actual city.

Of course, the crowning proof is the comment of Jesus Christ. Some think that, when Jesus referred to Jonah, he was using his characterization as an illustration as one would speak of Macbeth in Shakespeare—a fictional character made so vivid by his author that he seemed to be historical. We must judge for ourselves from the way Christ referred to him:

> For as Jonah was three days and three nights in the belly of a huge fish, so the Son of Man will be three days in the heart of the earth. The men of Nineveh will stand up at the judgment with this generation and condemn it; for they repented at the preaching of Jonah, and now one greater than Jonah is here [Matt. 12:40, 41, NIV].

If the repentant Ninevites are to be at the judgment to condemn the unrepentant Jerusalemites, I rather think there must have been some real preaching by a real prophet named Jonah.

Jesus spoke about Jonah several times in the New Testament. The village of Gath-Hepher, where Jonah lived in 800 B.C., was named Nazareth in later years. Jesus himself, therefore, grew up in Gath-Hepher or Nazareth. Undoubtedly, Jesus as a boy heard much about this prophet who was probably a local hero.

Jonah seemed to be quite familiar with the Psalms of David. Some think that the entire second chapter of Jonah was added to the story by a later author since the poetic form interrupts the narrative. This may be; yet, if the material of the story is historically accurate, it must have been written by someone who had access to Jonah's own writings. That Jonah was a writer we know. The prophecy of Jonah is said to be "from the hand" (not the mouth) of Jonah, meaning it was a written, rather than spoken, prophecy (2 Kings 14:25). If, therefore, source materials for the book came from Jonah, it is not unreasonable that after his escape, Jonah wrote in poetic or psalmic form his earnest prayers from the fish's belly. At any rate in Jonah's self-recorded prayer there is close resemblance to portions of the Psalms.

What does the Book of Jonah tell us besides its main point that God is not the exclusive property of any nation, that God is vitally concerned and compassionate toward all who will repent? Certainly, its meaning and interpretation are symbolical of the political and religious situation in Israel. As Professor William Graham states it:

> Let Jonah stand for the true Israel, Nineveh for paganism at its very worst, the sea for world politics, the vessel for diplomacy, the polyglot crew for the neighboring nations with which Israel

and Judah, to the disgust of the great prophets, were constantly intriguing, and the storm for the disturbance which shook the Near East when Babylon succeeded Assyria as the dominating power, and you have the main movements of thought and trend of events down to the Exile. The pre-Exilic prophets bear witness that their people constantly refused to trust and obey their own God, Jehovah, steadily turned away from their spiritual vocation and stubbornly preferred to work out their own destiny by means of diplomatic intrigue. History likewise witnesses that the nations in which Judah trusted for safety threw her overboard at last just as the sailors did Jonah.

Let the great fish stand for Babylon, Jonah's sojourn within it for the Exile, his miraculous deliverance for the freedom to return granted the exiles by Cyrus, emperor of the Medes and Persians and the chastened Jonah, who carried out his original commission to Nineveh, for the returning exiles who undertook the difficult task of transforming a paganized Palestine, and you have the main points of what actually happened in history down to the writer's own time.

From this point on the incidents of the

story typify the situation of his own day. The repentance of the Ninevites indicates the real desire of the native population to be counted good servants of Jehovah and their willingness to attempt ethical reforms. Jonah, sulking in his pitiful booth, grateful for the gourd, whining over its loss, stubbornly refusing to make God's merciful attitude to the heathen his own, is the Jewish congregation as the writer saw it, pining away in its shabby rebuilt Temple, looking for miraculous interventions on its own behalf, and stubbornly refusing to open its heart to the great heathen world outside through the salvation of which it could, alone, become great in the eyes of posterity and acceptable in the sight of God.

The denouement of the story of Jonah lies in the subsequent history of Assyria. For some unknown reason, in the latter half of King Adad-Nirari's reign, Assyria stopped her conquests and Israel regained the salvation of her country rather than being an aid to her enemies. Could it have been this great revival that stopped Nineveh? Some day we may know!

FIVE

Tempted to Be Angry with God
(Sin Number One)

If man is to know God, God must reveal himself to man. Through the Hebrews he did so. The Greeks were famous for architecture, beauty, athletics, and military prowess; the Romans were famous for law and empire; the Egyptians were famous for buildings, science, and medical discoveries.

The Hebrews were famous because God chose them as the means through which he would authoritatively reveal himself. That is why ancient books, written by Hebrews as far back as 1400 B.C. are still read with great interest by us today. The authentic self-revelation of God is found in those writings. This was the great "calling" that

God gave the Hebrews, who were described as a "chosen people."

Unfortunately, many of them later on thought they were a chosen people because they were inherently superior. God had said he chose them for a mission. To Abraham God promised, "Through your seed shall all the nations be blessed" (Gen. 22:18). The Jews grew clever and prosperous as a direct result of keeping the Mosaic law. But they also became a stiff-necked, stubborn people who willfully rejected God upon many occasions.

The Hebrews, not especially gifted in military matters, were defeated in battle about as often as they were victorious. Military prowess was not the purpose of their divine calling. God chose them for only one reason and that was to share the knowledge of God with the people of the world who had, as Paul said in Romans, corrupted the knowledge of God.

But they soon grew proud and began to boast, "We are the *chosen* people." They did not see that God's calling them to be a separated holy nation was only to prepare them for their mission of extending their faith to others. In fact, they wanted to keep to themselves the revelation which God had given to their prophets.

This error is what the Book of Jonah is

about. It is like a great sharp sword that pierces the heart of a nation with the tremendous truth that God cares for every race, every person, and his compassion should be shared especially by his own people. No one has the right to hold himself aloof and think himself better than others.

Christians are not to think they are "chosen" or superior. Rather, we are to open our hearts to share the gospel, and the love that it engenders, with a needy, lost, hurting world.

The Book of Jonah deals with God's concern for hurting people. The Ninevites, to whom Jonah went to preach, were sinners, as we all are. Their soldiers were known as among the cruelest people of the ancient world. When they conquered a city, one of their favorite practices was to make a pyramid of human skulls. Such horrible behavior is seen on their inscriptions now preserved in museums.

They had another delightful (to them) outdoor sport. Around a captured city, they would cut down trees, leaving a five-foot stump which they sharpened to a point. Then they would take their live captives and ram them down on those spikes and so rim the entire city with those impaled people. No wonder the poet Byron called them "the wolves of the nations." There was nothing we know that was very pleasant about this nation. Its people were generally hard, cruel and sadistic. Yet God wanted to forgive them. The way that he chose to do so was for one of his prophets to go to warn of judgment he would send if they did not change their evil ways.

God selected Jonah, the court prophet of northern Israel to be his messenger. God said "Jonah, go over there to Nineveh and tell those bloody-handed Assyrians that in forty days I am going to destroy their civilization."

Jonah rose up, the Bible says, to flee from the presence of the Lord and he went, not to the east, but as far toward the west as he could. He went down to Joppa first where he got on a boat to sail to Tarshish, in Spain.

But God prepared a great storm. The sailors recognized that it was supernatural in origin and sought for the man among them for whom the storm had been sent.

Jonah finally advised them, "Throw me into the sea; I am the sinner." So they threw him overboard. Can you imagine Jonah choosing to be thrown into the raging sea rather than to go to Nineveh!

Consequently, that stubborn man went down into the sea and then into a great sea monster which God had prepared. The whale went down to the bottom of the sea. After three days, Jonah repented and God caused the whale to throw him up on the land. So finally he went to Nineveh.

The fourth chapter tells us the story of what happened when he arrived. After Jonah preached to the Assyrians, surprisingly, they repented. God saw that they turned from their evil ways and he changed his mind about the promised judgment. This act of mercy greatly displeased Jonah and he became very angry. He prayed unto the Lord, "I pray thee, O Lord, was not this my saying when I was yet in my country? Therefore, I fled before unto Tarshish for I knew that thou art a gracious God, and merciful, slow to anger, and of great kindness, and repentest thee of this evil" (4:2).

Jonah, in other words, said, "I knew you were so good you would forgive those terrible Assryians. Lord, I told you so. I tried to escape from your commission. Now, Lord, take my life, for it is better for me to die than to live." Jonah was in a suicidal mood and full of self pity.

Then the Lord asked him, "Do you do well to be angry?"

Next Jonah went out of the city and sat on a hill overlooking the east side. There he made a booth for himself and sat under it in the shadow so that he might see what would become of the city. Perhaps Jonah still thought, "Maybe God *is* going to destroy Nineveh after all. I'll see." Then the Lord God prepared a gourd and made it come up over the booth to cover Jonah that it might be a shadow over his head. Jonah was very glad for the shade of the gourd.

In psychological terms, Jonah showed symptoms of being a "manic depressive," one whose feelings alternate violently up and down, a common ailment.

"Then God prepared a worm." (How many times when we seem reasonably happy, God prepares a *worm.*) When the sun rose the next day it smote the gourd and withered it. Then God prepared a violent east wind, and the sun beat upon the head of Jonah. He fainted and again wished to die.

Jonah felt compassion for the gourd. Then said the Lord, "Doest thou well to be angry for the gourd?"

Jonah answered, "I do well to be angry; I am justified in my anger, even unto death"—another expression of his death wish. He had asked to be thrown into the sea; he had told the Lord to kill him; now again he was asking death because of his anger.

Then the Lord said, "Thou hast had pity on the gourd, for the which thou hast not

laboured, neither madest it grow; which
came up in a night, and perished in a night:
And should not I spare Nineveh, that great
city, wherein are more than six score
thousand persons that cannot discern
between their right hand and their left?"
Nineveh was a tremendous city, with a
population of perhaps a half million or
more.

God did not ask, "Don't you feel sorry for
all those people who made those human
pyramids of human heads? Jonah, don't you
think you should feel sorry for those
people who impaled their captives and
extended their empire through blood?"
Instead, God spoke of their innocent little
children. He had asked, "Jonah, don't you
know that there are in Nineveh more than
one hundred and twenty thousand little
children who are not old enough to know
the difference between their right hand and
their left? You are feeling sorry for a *gourd*?
Don't you care about the innocent children?"
God rebuked him for his implacable, unmerci-
ful attitude.

This story of Jonah is about the temptation to be angry with God. We can't
say we haven't ever been angry with God,
because we probably have. Perhaps it
happened when we started a plan, or began
a new business. We may have found a new

friendship, or built a new home. Then something went wrong and we said, "God, if you exist, if you are a God of love, why did you let this happen?" So we became angry with God. All of us have, to some degree, been tempted to do this.

ANGER WITH GOD LEADS TO ATHEISM
Richard Wurmbrand in his book entitled *Was Karl Marx a Satanist?* demonstrates the strange truth that being angry with God is the real foundation of all atheism. No atheists in the world really started out in adulthood believing that God does not exist by simply examining the evidence. All of them at one time believed in God's existence, but in time they became angry with him for one reason or another and came to say to God, "I don't want you to interfere in my life, so I will convince myself that I don't believe in you and that will rid me of having to surrender to you." Or, "God, I don't like the way you are running this world, or my family or my life—I disagree with you, so I am going to believe you don't exist!" I have debated many atheists, including Madalyn Murray O'Hair, and I have consistently noted this trait.

An astonishing conversation took place

when the Soviet leader, Leonid Brezhnev, came to see President Carter about the SALT II Treaty. The first secretary of the Communist Party, the biggest atheistic movement on earth, said, "If America and Russia do not sign the SALT II Treaty, God will not forgive us!", as if all along he has and still does believe in God's existence!

Dr. Wurmbrand revealed how Karl Marx in his early youth was a member of a Christian church. His mother and father were Jews who had become Lutherans. When Marx was seventeen, he wrote a book he called *The Union of the Faithful with Christ*. One passage reads:

> Through the love of Christ, we turn our hearts at the same time toward our brethren who are inwardly bound to us, and for whom He gave Himself in sacrifice.

In another passage he wrote:

> Union with Christ could give an inner elevation, comfort in sorrow, calm trust, and a heart susceptible to human love, to everything noble and great, not for the sake of ambition and glory but only for the sake of Christ.

If one didn't know Karl Marx had written these words, it would be hard to believe it. Could this really be from the man who became such a great opponent to Christianity?

After Marx finished high school, he went to college to earn a doctorate in philosophy. During that time, a spiritual disaster overtook him. Historians aren't sure just what it was. Some suppose that Marx was praying for a scholarship or an honor that he didn't get. He really didn't need anything financially, for his parents were wealthy. His allowance was said to be larger than his teacher's salary. This man, who once professed faith in Christ, was not the child of an impoverished home.

His disappointment could have been from a love affair that didn't work out. Perhaps he prayed for some girl to marry him and she refused. Whatever it was that he prayed for, he didn't receive it. So at that crisis time in his life he wrote a poem in which he said, "I wish to avenge myself against the One who rules above."

It does not appear that he did not believe in the "One who rules above." He was just angry with him. Even though his parents supported him lavishly in his studies, he wrote: "A god has snatched from me my all. In the curse and rack of destiny, all his worlds have gone beyond recall, nothing but revenge is left for me."

Marx had very obviously learned a kind of Christianity which he knew with his head but not with his heart. He could write lovely poems and theological works about Christ, and then somehow turn on God in anger. Despite his understanding of the truth, he obviously had never surrendered his will to God. When God didn't do what he wanted him to do, Karl Marx said, "Only revenge is left for me."

Getting right with God doesn't just mean believing theologically on the Lord Jesus Christ. It means bending the knee and bowing the heart and surrendering the will to the living Son of God. The Christian should never allow anything to cause him to be angry with God. Disaster always follows our anger with God. All the suffering of the human race put together cannot equal the misery that has been caused by Karl Marx's communism. At least a hundred million people have been slain whose deaths can be traced to this system. Think also of the horror that has destroyed the liberties of so many nations. Think of the multitudes of hopes that were destroyed because this one man said to God, "I am going to take my vengeance on you." The Apostle James wrote: "How great a fire a little matter kindleth!" (James 3:5).

Some people haven't been in a church for a long time because they have been angry with God. That anger has not blessed their lives, or made them better people. It has soured them and prevented the power of God from flowing through their lives. They have become cynics, unbelievers, backsliders because of their anger.

CAN GOD DO WRONG?

Is anger with God ever justified? Paul wrote: "For what if some did not believe? shall their unbelief make the faith of God without effect? God forbid: yea, let God be true, but every man a liar" (Rom. 3:3, 4). Notice the expression, "Let God be true, but every man a liar." In other words, we can lie and rationalize, we can excuse ourselves, we can invent reasons why we sin or why we are justified in being angry with God. But there stands like a great Gibraltar this fact: "Let God be true, but every man a liar." In other words, our trust should be in God, not in human beings and their supposed reasons for being angry with God.

Paul wrote: "Nay but, O man, who art thou that repliest against God? Shall the thing formed say to him that formed it,

Why has thou made me thus? Hath not the potter power over the clay, of the same lump to make one vessel unto honour, and another unto dishonour?" (Rom. 9:20, 21).

The Greek word for "potter" is *kerameus*, from which we get our word "ceramics." God is the potter, who makes one lump of clay into a beautiful vase for the mantelpiece to hold roses; he makes another piece into a flower pot to hold ordinary plants. He makes one piece into a dish to set on the table and another into a vessel to feed the dog. People honor fancy vases more than they do flower pots. So it is with God. He has a right to do with his clay whatever he wishes. He then asks, "But who are you, O man, to talk back to God?" (Rom. 9:20, NIV). The whole point of Paul's illustration is that God is sovereign.

The Bible tells of many people who were tempted to be angry with God. But Abraham the father of faith made a statement about God that is as true today as it was four thousand years ago when he asked the rhetorical question: "Shall not the Judge of all the earth do right?" (Gen. 18:25).

When we are tempted to blame God or say, "Lord, you don't know what you are doing with me because you are causing me to suffer, you have neglected me, you've been unkind to me, and Lord, I am angry with you," we should remember Abraham. He didn't know Jesus, or have the Bible to help him, but he correctly understood, "Shall not the Judge of all the earth do right?"

It is the inherent nature of God to be good. Some so-called theologians have postulated that the God of the Old Testament might even be termed "sadistic." But Abraham knew better when he said, "Shall not the Judge of all the earth do right?"

We need that truth when the tears start coursing down our cheeks, when the doors are slammed in our faces, when a faithful friend betrays us, when we are criticized at a time we don't deserve it. If we are guided by heavenly wisdom, we are instead going to look up and say, "Lord, I am tempted to be angry with you, but shall not the Judge of all the earth do right?" That attitude is part of what is meant when the Bible says, "Abraham believed God, and it was accounted to him for righteousness" (Gal. 3:6; Gen. 15:6).

DOES GOD FORBID OUR QUESTIONS?
God forbids us to be angry with him because anger is an imputation of blame. As has been mentioned, anger toward God

is the parent of all unbelief and atheism. The Bible puts it this way, "He that cometh to God must believe that he is, and that he is a rewarder of them that diligently seek him" (Heb. 11:6). Those truths are the foundation of prayer. We must believe that he exists and that he rewards. In other words, that he is good and that he responds to prayer.

But what about our legitimate questions? Does God welcome an honest question? The prophet Habakkuk admitted that he was angry with God. Then he thought better of it and decided instead just to ask God some questions about his consistency. Though he was a bit afraid of what God would reply, he decided to ask anyway.

> O Lord, how long shall I cry, and thou wilt not hear! even cry out unto thee of violence, and thou wilt not save! Why dost thou shew me iniquity and cause me to behold grievance? for spoiling [the spoils of war; the consequences of invasion] and violence are before me: and there are that raise up strife and contention. Therefore the law is slacked, and judgment doth never go forth: for the wicked doth compass about the righteous; therefore wrong judgment proceedeth [Hab. 1:2-4].

Everywhere this prophet looked he saw things happening that should not happen if God, as he claimed, was in control. He continued:

> Thou art of purer eyes than to behold evil, and canst not look on iniquity: wherefore lookest thou upon them that deal treacherously, and holdest thy tongue when the wicked devoureth the man that is more righteous than he? [Hab. 1:13]

In effect, Habakkuk was saying, "Lord, I've been taught from your Word that you are so pure that you can't look upon evil, but, Lord, I look around me and see evil, and you've got to see what I see. Now, Lord, I want to know why? What are you up to?"

Then the prophet said, "I will stand upon my watch, and set me upon the tower, and will watch to see what he will say unto me, and what I shall answer when I am reproved" (Hab. 2:1). He seemed to know that God was going to reprove him, but just the same, he was going to ask.

Habakkuk was faced with the intellectual question about why wrong triumphed and virtue lay in the dust, why God permitted the existence of evil. This is one of the most profound theological questions in the world.

The Lord answered Habakkuk, "Write the vision, and make it plain upon tables, that he may run that readeth it. For the vision is yet for an appointed time, but at the end it shall speak, and not lie; though it tarry, wait for it; because it will surely come, it will not tarry" (Hab. 2:2, 3). God was saying, "I don't settle my accounts on Saturday night. I take time to work out my judgments. So be patient."

Next we read the statement so often quoted in the New Testament: "Behold, his soul that is lifted up is not upright in him: but the just shall live by his faith" (Hab. 2:4). The last half of this little verse was the great answer that God gave the prophet. In effect, he said, "Habakkuk, if you've got a question as to why I don't kill the wicked, or justify the righteous; if you ask what I'm doing about evil, then let me tell you, be patient. I haven't settled everything yet, but I will. You are to wait for it. In the meantime, the just shall live by his faith."

We could say, "Karl Marx, you were angry at God, but you shouldn't have been. In the meantime, the just shall live by faith." We must have confidence in God himself, in his purpose and plan, confidence that God knows what he is doing, confidence in his character and goodness. But Karl Marx refused to do this and unleashed much evil upon himself and the world.

We all face cruel disappointments. We cry to God and he responds in his Word, "Just wait a while—be patient. Someday it will work out and in the meantime, the just shall live by faith."

When Augustine faced the gathering clouds of the Dark Ages, he wrote his confessions on the theme, "The just shall live by faith." After the long dark night of the Middle Ages, when God transformed the heart of Martin Luther, the heart of the reformation was Luther's rediscovery of the truth, "The just shall live by faith."

Do not think this truth is only for theologians like Paul, Augustine, and Luther. It is for ordinary people who are in trouble and suffering. We have a choice. We can be angry at God or we can be one of the just who live by faith.

SIX

Tempted to Have a Hard Heart
(Sin Number Two)

The Prophet Jonah committed seven great sins. It is easy for us to look back now through history and try to reconstruct a clear view of his failures. But to dwell too long upon Jonah's sins is to make a mistake, because what we should see is that the same sins are still prevalent among us. We should say, "These are my sins I am reading about—not Jonah's alone. I thank God that he preserved this story of Jonah's sins, not to disgrace this great man, but that God might speak eloquently out of the prophet's experience to my need to avoid the same great sins which so easily captured Jonah."

A number of very important truths are

presented in the closing verses of Jonah's magnificent story (3:5—4:11). Among other things, it is a classic of a heart grown hard.

JESUS AND FORGIVENESS

In the New Testament, Jesus told a similar story about a man who had incurred a great debt (Matt. 18:23-35). He apparently had made an unwise investment on behalf of his master who owned much property. This man might possibly have been a slave, since slaves in that day were often given positions of great importance and responsibility. Whether servant or slave, this man made an investment of his master's wealth without the master's permission and lost a great sum of money. It was a staggering debt, opening the servant to the charge of embezzlement or mismanagement. He had no way to repay the money, so he came and prostrated himself before his master and said, "I have lost your money." The Bible says that the master forgave him the enormous debt.

The same servant went out and found a man who owed him a handful of coins and he said to his fellow servant, "You owe me that money. Pay me now, or else!" The other servant explained that he was sorry but that he couldn't pay the money. So the first servant had him thrown into jail.

The master heard of this terrible behavior and brought before him the first servant whom he had forgiven so much, and said, "I have forgiven you this great debt and yet you turn around and treat with such severity a person who owes you a comparatively minor amount. I am going to put your debt back upon you and you are going to prison. You are not going to come out until you pay the very last coin."

This story is in some ways a restatement of the story of Jonah and his hard heart. Jonah had been forgiven for breaking his vows, yet he would not proclaim forgiveness to the Assyrians. To be a prophet, Jonah had to vow that he would proclaim the Word of God—not change it—but fearlessly, obediently proclaim it whenever he was called upon by God to do so. But Jonah had refused and had abandoned his calling and had run away. Instead of going to Nineveh, he took a ship in the opposite direction. Only after three days in the whale's belly did the stubborn prophet pray, "Lord, I will pay my vows."

Immediately, God forgave him and had the fish throw him up on the shore. At last, Jonah reluctantly gave Nineveh the message of warning, and God brought the great spiritual awakening. Then Jonah immediately became very angry about this extension of God's mercy.

Could you imagine a doctor of medicine, a servant of the health of the people, becoming angry when he is asked to save someone's life? Can you imagine a statesman called to head a government, when he is presented with a great challenge to the security of the nation, becoming angry that he is being asked to serve his country? Can you imagine a school teacher who has the knowledge to share with pupils becoming angry when he or she is asked to teach the children?

If you were God, what would you think of a man who is asked to do something that he has promised in advance that he will do, but becomes angry when he is asked to do it? In Jonah's case it was even worse, since his task involved the welfare of many innocent people.

That Jonah could feel sorry for the gourd and yet have no compassion on innocent children and animals is incredible. "One hundred and twenty thousand who do not know between their right hand and their left," was a picturesque way of saying, "innocent children." The prophet of God seemed not to care even for little children, so deep was his anger. Nor did he care for the innocent people who didn't share in the

sins of the soldiers and the king of
Nineveh.

Chapter four reveals that Jonah, being a
man of God—standing as he did in the
great tradition of Elijah and Elisha—was
not ignorant of what God was like. Part of
the Bible was written by the time of Jonah,
so he was responsible for knowing it. As
early as the eighth century before Christ,
there was among God's people some
understanding of the universality of God's
plan to save the whole world. The fact that
we have the Book of Jonah in the Bible is
an indication that perhaps Jonah, after the
experience was over, wrote about his own
experience. Whether or not he wrote the
book which bears his name, he must have
left an account of some kind or we would
not have known what took place.

We can only hope that Jonah came out
all right in the end—that he finally understood God's point. The fact that he recorded
these things about himself is some evidence
that he did. But we are certain Jonah really
did know what God was like. Jonah himself
confessed that he knew about God and his
nature. "I knew that thou art a gracious
God, and merciful, slow to anger, and of
great kindness, and repentest thee of
the evil" (4:2).

It could accurately be said that Jonah

was one of God's principal agents on earth at the time. Furthermore, he knew what God had called him to preach; not only God's judgment but God's forgiveness, love, and mercy. Moreover, Jonah himself had been forgiven a hideous wrong which he had committed against God in forsaking his prophetic calling and defying God.

In spite of having been forgiven, he was angry with God and hardened his heart when God went about his great purpose, that of saving souls.

THE PHARISEES,
THE PRIESTS, AND THE BLIND MAN

In the New Testament, there is another story about the "Jonah attitude"—another story of hardheartedness. There was a man who was born blind. A blind baby is a pitiful sight. So much of life a blind child is never going to experience. But, this one grew to adulthood and then Jesus came along and gave him sight. When the priests and Pharisees heard about it, they did not say, "Oh, this is wonderful! You were born blind and now you can see. Congratulations! Welcome to the world of sight! How did it happen? Tell us about it!" Instead, they tried to force witnesses to say that Jesus, the healer of the blind man, was a charlatan.

Then they summoned the man himself

and demanded to know the truth. So he
explained how Jesus had healed him. But
they didn't believe it. At last they called
him again. "How did he open your eyes?"
Again he told them, but they did not heed.
They said, "We are disciples of Moses. We
know that God spoke to Moses, but as for
this fellow, we don't even know where he
comes from" (John 9:29, NIV).

The man replied that Jesus must have
come from God, or God would not have
heard his prayer for healing. This made the
Pharisees angry. They shouted, "How dare
you lecture us?" Then they threw him out
of the temple.

These official religious leaders, like
Jonah, were so full of religion, law-keeping,
and self-righteousness that they were
actually angry when a sufferer was divinely
healed. They discounted the healing because Jesus did it without their authority.
That is the "Jonah spirit"—the spirit of
hardheartedness.

If it was possible for Jonah to be that
hardhearted, and if it was possible for the
Pharisees to be that way, be very sure that
it is also possible for us to be hardhearted
too.

We are frequently tempted to play God
by judging others. If we could only be
tempted instead to imitate God's redemp-

tive attitudes! God is a redeemer, and we should be like him—we should imitate his forgiveness. But he forbids us to imitate him as a judge. We are eager to be judges, but we don't seem to like to bear the message of forgiveness and redemption. We are like Jonah when we have a hard heart toward being redemptive to others.

THE HARDENED HEART IS NEVER JUSTIFIED

God is busy about the task of redeeming people. Some may object and say, "But people are not worth it. They are no good." They are correct! That is what the Bible keeps saying, "There is none righteous, no, not one" (Ps. 5:9; Rom. 3:10). "All have sinned and come short of the glory of God" (Rom. 3:23), including us.

Someone reports, "People are unresponsive," yet, how many times have we been asked to take a church job and we found an excuse to say no?

"People let you down!" Of course they do—just like we do, because we are human beings with feet of clay. We are all flawed. Anything we can say about other people, someone can usually correctly say about us.

There are some who say, "I don't want to get involved in trying to reach people because I will fail. People will respond for a while but they will soon slip away." Certainly, people fail God. No one ever talks about how Jesus also failed, but he experienced even this for us. He seemed to fail with Judas and the rich young ruler. Once in awhile, Jesus failed with his apostles—not through any fault of his, but because he was dealing with flawed human nature. But, in the end, our Lord Jesus Christ accomplished exactly what God sent him to do. He secured what the Bible called, "his remnant."

FAILINGS OR NOT, GOD WILL SUCCEED

In the Book of Acts, we see very plainly what God's purpose for the world and the Church are: "God is drawing out of all nations a people for his name" (Acts 15:14). There will of course be some Judases, there will be some rich young rulers, some who will escape through his fingers because they have never allowed themselves to be placed in the hollow of God's hand.

When life and Christian service are over, God will have two things which will survive: the remnant—those that God redeemed—and the accomplishment of having done something wonderful to us in the process of using us in redeeming other people. In helping to redeem others, we ourselves will have grown in grace and the knowledge of the Lord Jesus Christ, and therefore be fitted to help God rule his universe.

We Christians belong to Christ and to his Church irretrievably. There are no ways out; there are no escape clauses. Like all others, we are sinners saved by grace. We can say with all our hearts, "I know whom I have believed, and am persuaded that he is able to keep that which I have committed unto him against that day" (2 Tim. 1:12).

Along the way, we may at times slip and fall. But that is not reason for a modern-day Christian "Jonah" to close his mind and harden his heart against us. Like the Ninevites, we may need restoration. Paul said, "Brethren, if a man be overtaken in a fault, ye which are spiritual, restore such an one in the spirit of meekness; considering thyself, lest thou also be tempted" (Gal. 6:1). Jonah could not face that requirement and keep a hardened heart. Neither can we nor any other real child of God.

SEVEN
Tempted
to Be Stubborn
(Sin Number Three)

Jesus referred to the first chapter of Jonah as he was speaking about his own death and resurrection. "As Jonas was three days and three nights in the whale's belly; so shall the son of man be three days and three nights in the bowels of the earth" (Matt. 12:40).

Thus, Jesus testified to the historicity of Jonah's great experience. But the story is more than history. It is a mirror held up to life.

The city in which Jonah was born in 725 B.C., then called Gath-Hepher, in the first century before Christ came to be known as Nazareth. Jonah was the only

prophet who came from Nazareth besides
the Lord Jesus Christ. Jonah's book, therefore, was known by Jesus from the human
standpoint as well as from the divine. It
is not unlikely that Jonah was considered
a hometown hero.

The story told how Jonah found himself
in the midst of a great storm which the
Lord had prepared. Jonah could very easily
have stopped that storm by repenting, but
he didn't. Instead, he stubbornly insisted,
"Throw me overboard." In other words, he
would rather die than give in to what
God wanted him to do! So much human
terror and suffering are suggested in the
words: "And Jonah was in the belly of the
fish three days and three nights" (1:17).
How easy to narrate but how hideous to
have experienced it! A great sea monster
with its jaws open wide approaches and
there is no way to escape. You had
thought you were going to drown but
instead you find you are going to be
eaten! Suddenly the enormity of your fate
bursts upon you.

If Jonah cried out to God, it wasn't
recorded. He apparently accepted his fate
without a word. One might have supposed
that was to be the end of Jonah. Jonah
himself must have thought that, but still
he did not repent. As the hours went by,

Jonah was probably surprised to find that he was able to breathe in that restricted place. It must have been terribly smelly, very damp, and awfully dark, accompanied by a dizzying sensation as the whale swam around.

The first day went by. By that time, surely Jonah must have been living in terror. Yet, he still didn't repent. A second day went by. By then he had probably lost all track of time. Fitfully dozing, expecting never to wake up, still he didn't repent.

Three days went by. The sea monster went down to the bottom of the sea to feel better, but that didn't do it for him. So the whale began to eat seaweed, which is what we are told a whale would do naturally if something ailed him. But this time it didn't help.

After three days and three nights, Jonah finally gave in and said, "I have been chastened enough—I'm going to change."

The Bible tells the story:

From inside the fish Jonah prayed to the Lord his God. He said: "In my distress I called to the Lord, and he answered me. From the depths of the grave, I called for help, and you listened to my cry. You hurled me into the deep, into the very heart of the seas, and the currents swirled about me; all your waves and breakers swept over me. I said, 'I have been banished from your sight; yet I will look again toward your holy temple.' The engulfing waters threatened me; seaweed was wrapped around my head. To the roots of the mountains I sank down; the earth beneath barred me in forever. But you brought my life up from the pit, O Lord my God. When my life was ebbing away, I remembered you, Lord, and my prayer rose to you, to your holy temple. Those who cling to worthless idols forfeit the grace that could be theirs. But I, with a song of thanksgiving will sacrifice to you. What I have vowed I will make good. Salvation comes from the Lord." And the Lord commanded the fish, and it vomited Jonah onto dry land [2:1-10, NIV].

This is the most vivid story in the Bible of a man of God whose sin was stubbornness. We stand back in amazement at this man and marvel that he was so stubborn. When I have sinned, it has never taken nearly that much to break me. Not Jonah! He was willing to die in the sea by drowning rather than do the will of God. He crossed off his life. He thought, "The earth is about me forever, the waters encompassed me about." It took three ghastly days and nights to get him to pray, "Lord, I will pay my vows."

There is a principle in this verse that follows every one of us. When, for instance, we attempt to pray, but instantly become aware of a sin in our lives, we recall the Word of God which says, "If I regard iniquity in my heart, the Lord will not hear me" (Ps. 66:18). When the sin comes right up in our minds we first try to ignore it. We may attempt to rationalize it, to explain it away, or make an excuse for it. But it keeps popping up.

We may ask God to bless us in a new enterprise we are starting, or even in a new task for him, but we sense uneasily that God's blessing isn't on us. Immediately we know why. Because there is one place in our lives which is not yielded to God. We may begin to try to reason with God: "Lord, I'll give you everything else you want, but let me hold onto that one thing."

If there is a room in our hearts, in our lives, in our practices, in our habits, in our friendships which God cannot enter, Jesus then is not really our King.

God had said to Jonah, "Go to Nineveh." Jonah must have replied to the Lord, "I can serve you perfectly well right here in Samaria where I am the court prophet to the king. Just think of the importance of my role today." But God had said, "Go to Nineveh."

When Jonah decided to run away and went to Joppa to take a ship for Tarshish, he might have thought, "Lord, Tarshish is a great city of opportunity; there are ships going from there to all the ports of western Europe. Just think of the missionary openings I'll have over there. You want me to be a missionary to Nineveh. But I can't stand those Ninevites. But Lord, if I go to Tarshish, just think of all the people I can reach for you! They desperately need a prophet there." Jonah may have thought that if he reached Tarshish far away from the scene of his calling God might send someone else to Nineveh and forget about him for the time being.

If there is a place in our hearts that we won't give up, a habit, a friendship, or something God has placed his finger upon, which every time we pray comes up in our minds, it is with us as it was with Jonah. God had said, "Go to Nineveh." Jonah resisted and argued. Finally he defied God, "Lord, I would rather die than preach in Nineveh!"

God never asks anything of us except for our own good, but he seems always to ask the one thing that we don't want to do.

God told Abraham to sacrifice his son
Isaac. The Bible reveals that God, of course
was never in favor of human sacrifice.
Nevertheless, God had to persuade Abraham
to place his precious son on the altar. God,
however, in advance, had prepared a ram as
a substitute. Nevertheless, Isaac was the
one he asked for.

Abraham must have thought, "Lord, I
have a whole drove of camels over there, I
have a flock of sheep and a herd of donkeys.
Couldn't I sacrifice any one of them
instead? Lord, anything but Isaac; he is the
only son I have. He is the one through
whom your promises were given to me that
I'll be a blessing to the nations." But God
insisted, "I want Isaac."

Abraham must have had a stubborn
struggle with God, but he finally took Isaac
to the altar. Then God brought the
substitutionary ram at the moment when
he had made Abraham's heart willing to
sacrifice Isaac.

The feelings of God about stubbornness
are told in the words of Samuel the prophet
to King Saul: "For rebellion is as the sin of
witchcraft, and stubbornness is as iniquity
and idolatry. Because thou hast rejected the
word of the Lord, he hath rejected thee
from being king" (1 Sam. 15:23).

One might as well worship an idol as to

be stubborn. There was no sin referred to in the Old Testament times that God judged more severely than the worship of idols. In the New Testament, Paul described the worship of idols as the worship of demons (1 Cor. 10:20), yet God said stubbornness is just as bad.

Why do we resist God's Word and God's directives? Why do we say we won't obey? There are at least five common reasons:

1. We may actually not realize the difference between determination and stubbornness. The world has been built, civilization advanced, and Christianity blessed by men of great determination because it is somewhat akin to faith. Determination is a virtue because it is shown in faith or reliance upon God. Stubbornness is sinful because it is mere self-reliance and does not consider the will of God as the goal.

2. We resist God because we seem to think we know what is best for us. Such thinking borders on blasphemy. I knew a lot of answers when I was a young preacher of twenty. I have found out that I didn't know as much as I thought. But one thing I know is that what God wants for me is best. His will is best for him, best for the kingdom, and it is best for each of us.

Sometimes we think that God is unreasonably asking a particular thing of us because as far as we can see, it will "ruin everything." We might say, "Lord, I've got a great romance going, but if I give her (or him) up, it will ruin everything." Still, God sometimes insists, "Give up the romance."

"Lord, I've got some business plans and I just wish you would bless me. If you will bless me. I will tithe." But down in our hearts we may know that God doesn't want us in that particular enterprise. God says, "Give it up." For example, God may actually be trying to prevent bankruptcy for us, but we don't see ahead. God may be preventing us from some other terrible thing he knows will overtake us, some accident that is inevitable if we continue to be stubborn.

God, who sees the future and loves us totally, knows what is best for us.

3. Pride is a socially accepted sin, but it is an abomination in the sight of God. Pride is the mother of all sins. Murder springs from pride; theft springs from pride. When we decide to serve God on our own terms, then at that moment pride has substituted our will for God's will.

Jonah was most willing to serve God in Samaria, on his own terms. Jonah was not an atheist, nor an unbeliever; Jonah was not a man who engaged in what we would call social sins. He was a good, virtuous man. But he had the sin of pride, and consequently the sin of stubbornness. In effect God had also said, "I don't want you in Tarshish. That's no sacrifice as far as I am concerned. I want you to serve me in Nineveh as I told you."

God had to break Jonah's pride. Some may ask, "Does God always do things that are so painful to us when we don't yield our pride?" Yes, if he has to. The Bible says, "We are chastened of the Lord, that we should not be condemned with the world" (1 Cor. 11:32). Elsewhere it is recorded: "For whom the Lord loveth he chasteneth, and scourgeth every son whom he receiveth" (Heb. 11:6).

If we persist in stubbornness, God will first convict us of our sins inwardly. Second, he will put a blanket over our prayers so that they will not be answered. Third, he will send small troubles our way. Fourth, if all that doesn't work, he will send enormous troubles until he gets us to bow our heads and bend our knees, just as Jonah eventually had to do. Jonah's story appears in the Bible for our welfare and warning.

4. We resist God through our stubbornness because we deceive ourselves. Jonah eventually admitted that. When he finally

did repent, he had this verdict to pronounce upon his own sins: "They that observe lying vanities forsake their own mercy" (2:8).

This is saying that when we are influenced and guided by an empty lie, we are cutting off our own way out. This does not refer to eternal salvation but to salvation in a given perilous situation.

5. We are stubborn because we are disobedient. "He, that being often reproved hardeneth his neck, shall suddenly be destroyed, and that without remedy" (Prov. 29:1). The way out for Jonah was repentance, but he chose stubbornness.

God must have said to him when he was a younger man, "I want you to be a prophet." So Jonah made a vow that every prophet of God must make, even to this day. He probably said something like this:

> O God, I will speak the truth. I will never claim as the Word of the Lord that which is only my own wisdom. I will faithfully proclaim thy Word. I will go where you want me to go; I'll say what you want me to say.

Preachers who are earnest and sincere have always made vows similar to that.

Jonah had broken all aspects of the

prophet's vow. But finally he bowed down his head before God in that whale's stomach and said, "Lord, I'll go. I'll pay my vows."

Whatever we have promised to do, whatever we have vowed to God that we would perform, remember that part of overcoming the sin of stubbornness is to repent, meaning to change direction, to change the mind. Before God chastened us we may have been unwilling to pay our vows. Now after the chastening we are willing and are on our way back, through repentance, to God's forgiveness and restoration.

In spite of God's severe chastening, God was tender to Jonah. The very moment that Jonah repented, God sent the fish to the shore near Joppa and Jonah was released. "The Lord spoke to the fish and it vomited out Jonah on dry land" (2:10). God didn't keep him down there any longer than it took to break him.

FOUR PREPARED THINGS

God prepared many things as this story reveals. When Jonah became stubborn, God prepared a storm, not to overwhelm Jonah or to kill him, but to bring him to his senses.

Jonah was still stubborn. So God prepared a fish. But God was still in control, because the fish delivered Jonah right where God wanted him to be. God prepared the city of Nineveh so that when Jonah arrived there he was received.

Whatever brought out the crowd, we do know the Bible says the whole city of Nineveh repented. Everybody may have flocked out just to see this man who for three days and three nights had been in the whale. From the king's house right down to the lowest donkey, they wore sackcloth and ashes on their heads as a sign of repentance. That great city turned wholly to God.

God gave Jonah a magnificent commission to go and bring awakening to the city of Nineveh. This had been God's prepared plan all along. God didn't want to hurt Jonah or chastise him. He wanted him to be the means of the greatest revival in history. Yet, Jonah, in the face of that glorious opportunity, was stubborn.

The greatest miracle in the story of Jonah was not the gourd that God prepared, which grew overnight and formed a shelter from the sun, nor the storm, nor the whale. Nor was it even Jonah's preservation. The greatest miracle in the Book of Jonah was

the spiritual awakening of the city of
Nineveh. God's hand was always present at
every stage. When he had to be severe, he
was, and yet he was always tender, always
redemptive, always moving toward a
solution.

It is the same for us today. The Bible
tells us in Paul's words:

> But let a man examine himself, and so
> let him eat of that bread, and drink of
> that cup. For he that eateth and drinketh
> unworthily, eateth and drinketh damna-
> tion to himself, not discerning the Lord's
> body. For this cause many are weak and
> sickly among you, and many sleep. For if
> we would judge ourselves, we should not
> be judged [1 Cor. 11:28-31].

The writer of the Epistle to the Hebrews
wrote:

> And you have forgotten the exhortation
> which speaketh unto you as unto
> children, My son, despise not thou the
> chastening of the Lord, nor faint when
> thou art rebuked of him: For whom the
> Lord loveth he chasteneth, and scourgeth
> every son whom he receiveth. If ye
> endure chastening, God dealeth with you

as with sons; for what son is he whom
the father chasteneth not? [Heb. 12:5-7]

Later he wrote:

Now no chastening for the present
seemeth to be joyous, but grievous:
nevertheless afterward it yieldeth the
peaceable fruit of righteousness unto
them which are exercised thereby [Heb.
12:11].

That was Jonah. God loved him and dealt
with him severely and then tenderly when
he called him again to go to Nineveh.
I must live by the truth or be chastened
by it, just as you must. What is God saying
to us today? Is there a decision he wants us
to make? Maybe we have thought a lot
about becoming a Christian but have put it
off. Now we know more of what God is
like and requires than we did before
learning about God and Jonah. As Christians we may need to say, "Lord, I have
been as stubborn as Jonah. I am going to
give it up." Then, do it.

EIGHT

Tempted to Give God Less Than Our Best
(Sin Number Four)

A. B. Simpson, the founder of the Christian and Missionary Alliance, was a great poet and hymn writer. Some of his hymns are still used. One of his most famous was titled "God's Best."

> *God has His best*
> *   for the few who dare to stand the test.*
> *God has His second best*
> *   for those who will not have His best.*

Jonah was a great man, but yet a man who could have been greater had he given God his very best. In the third chapter of his book, we see what happened to him after the whale threw him up on dry land.

And the word of the Lord came unto Jonah the second time, saying, Arise, go unto Nineveh, that great city, and preach unto it the preaching that I bid thee. So Jonah arose, and went unto Nineveh, according to the word of the Lord. Now Nineveh was an exceeding great city of three days' journey. And Jonah began to enter into the city a day's journey, and he cried, and said, yet forty days, and Nineveh shall be overthrown [3:1-4].

It is so much better for us when we respond to God the first time he speaks. Jonah had to receive his commission a second time, because he was not willing to give God his best. Instead, he gave God just enough to get by. That was one of Jonah's sins.

At least Jonah did not preach what we call the social gospel. Nineveh was an ideal place to preach social reform, because the Ninevites were among the worst behaved people that ever lived. But reform was not nearly enough and Jonah knew it.

He was faithful in that he preached exactly the message God had given him. Biblical preaching doesn't give anyone an excuse to be lazy or fail to adequately

prepare our messages. We should preach
"Thus saith the Lord."

Jonah did not have to put much
preparation into his sermon. He didn't
have to organize an evangelistic team.
There is no word that he hired a singer
and an advance man, or anybody to
arrange interviews. He just went into
town, stood up, and gave the message to
the Ninevites. But his sermon does appear
to be a rather half-hearted, grudging kind of
message. The lesson is obvious. God was
eager to redeem the people of Nineveh, so
he brought about a great revival despite the
half-hearted efforts of Jonah.

How was his half-hearted effort shown?
First of all, God had to send him twice.
The second time, he went into the city
and preached only of judgment to come.
When he was finished, he gave the
impression that he couldn't wait for the
brimstone and fire to start falling. "And
God saw their works, that they turned
from their evil way; and God repented of
the evil, that he had said that he would
do unto them; and he did it not" (3:10).
But Jonah didn't like it. "It displeased
Jonah exceedingly, and he was very angry"
(4:1).

Jonah had been chosen by God to do
a job that became historic. The largest

crowd of people ever gathered on the face of the earth, as far as we know, met in Korea to hear Billy Graham. It numbered slightly over one million people. But if there has ever been an arousal of spiritual concern of the nature and size of that which happened to Nineveh, we don't know about it. This was without question one of the greatest evangelistic campaigns in history.

Suppose that God had chosen you to be his evangelist for an occasion like this. Suppose that he had been preparing you for it all your life. I don't think you would want to run from that great moment. But Jonah did!

If you knew what God was going to do with you, would you drag your feet? I think you would want to give God your best. But not Jonah—he was unyielding. His prejudices and his stubborn will were more important to him than doing the will of God.

Jonah was a genuine prophet, a man of God. But he was half-hearted. In other words, he didn't achieve God's best for his life. As we examine the Old Testament, we see some evidence that makes his reluctance even harder to understand.

According to the Old Testament, Jonah was the first prophet to appear on the

scene after the death of Elisha. First came
Elijah, the great prophet. Then he, in turn,
was succeeded by his servant and co-
minister, Elisha, a man completely "sold out"
for God. When Elisha was called to be a
prophet, he was plowing a field with a yoke
of oxen as Elijah came looking for him. He
walked over to Elisha and took off his
mantle and threw it over Elisha. Elisha
must have been a man of keen perception
to understand the significance of this
gesture. He realized that he was being
called to succeed the prophetic office of
Eiljah, so the young man returned to his
home. He called in his people and told
them he was going to be a prophet. He
kissed his mother and father and left, never
looking back. In fact, he slew the oxen and
used the plow and harnesses for firewood
and provided a farewell banquet for his
family, saying symbolically, "I am giving up
everything to fulfill my call to be a prophet.
I'm burning all my bridges."

Many years later, Elisha said to Elijah,
"My master, upon your leaving this life, I
desire a double portion of thy spirit,"
meaning, "I want twice as much power
with God as you have had." Elijah then
promised, "If you see me go, you can have a
double portion of my spirit."

The two traveled to the Jordan River and

Elijah, to test Elisha, said, "Stay on this side of the river; I am going across the Jordan to pray." Elisha responded, "I will go with you." Evidently, he didn't want the old prophet out of his sight, because he didn't want to miss the double portion of blessing.

Later, they walked on into the plain of Jordan at the spot about where the Allenby Bridge stands today, where people cross over from Israel into Jordan. Suddenly Elijah was caught up to heaven and his mantle, his cloak, fell down to the ground. Elisha took it up and went back down to the Jordan River. He smote the waters of the river with Elijah's mantle and cried, "Where is the Lord God of Elijah?" The waters parted and he went over on dry land to the other side, showing him that he had received his request for God's blessing.

What was Elisha like? He was willing to be totally dedicated to God's service. In all the Bible, there isn't a single word of reproof against him from God. He was a man who lived for God one hundred percent.

Jonah succeeded this man, Elisha, who had set him a fine example. We have no record, but Jonah could well have been one of the men who studied with Elijah and Elisha in the school of the prophets in Gilgal. At least we know that Jonah knew

some of the stories about Elisha, such as
this story recorded about him:

Now Elisha was suffering from the
illness from which he died. Jehoash king
of Israel went down to see him and wept
over him. "My father! My father!" he
cried. "The chariots and horsemen of
Israel!" Elisha said, "Get a bow and some
arrows," and he did so. "Take the bow in
your hands," he said to the king of Israel.
When he had taken it, Elisha put his
hands on the king's hands. "Open the
east window," he said, and he opened it.
"Shoot!" Elisha said, and he shot. "The
Lord's arrow of victory, the arrow of
victory over Aram!" Elisha declared. "You
will completely destory the Arameans at
Aphek." Then he said, "Take the arrows,"
and the king took them. Elisha told him,
"Strike the ground." He struck it three
times and stopped. The man of God was
angry with him and said, "You should
have struck the ground five or six times;
then you would have defeated Aram and
completely destroyed it. But now you will
defeat it only three times" [2 Kings
13:14-19, NIV].

Elisha told him that the bow and arrows
had a symbolic meaning: "This is the bow

of the Lord," and "This is the arrow of the Lord's deliverance." He prophesied, "You are going to defeat the enemies of Israel who have cruelly ground them under their heels."

The last event in the life of Elisha was this drama of the bow and arrows. The prophet was angry because the king had been half-hearted. The king did not have his whole mind in the job that was his as king, to deliver his nation from the foreign oppressor. To humor the old prophet, he struck the floor with arrows just three times, somewhat lackadaisically. As king and war leader, he was with a prophet who had been mightily used of God in national matters. Elisha had warned him that the arrows actually represented God's deliverance. He told him that the bow represented his kingship under God. In spite of knowing the symbolism of the weaponry,
he struck the ground only three times. Elisha was disappointed. The king should have struck five or six times. Now he was going to have only three victories because of his half-heartedness.

Elisha died and was succeeded several years later by Jonah as the official court prophet in Israel. Jonah could not have helped knowing that story of the bow and arrows, the king and the victories, because he was right there on the scene. Jonah probably witnessed the three victories. He at least knew about them. He had heard and seen the object lesson of the peril of half-hearted service to God. The final lesson from the life of Elisha was the very one that Jonah failed to learn himself.

Jonah also knew about Caleb who lived long before him. Caleb and Joshua were two of the twelve spies that Moses sent to spy out the promised land. When they came back, Joshua and Caleb told Moses and the people of Israel, "We should go up and take possession of the land, for we can certainly do it" (Nim. 13:30, NIV).

But the other ten spies were saying: "'We can't attack those people; they are stronger than we are.' And they spread among the Israelites a discouraging report about the land they had explored. They said, 'The land we explored devours those living in it. All the people we saw there are of great size'" (Num. 13:31, 32, NIV).

As a result of their unbelief, God said to Moses: "Not one of the men who saw my glory and the miraculous signs I performed in Egypt and in the desert but who disobeyed me and tested me ten times—not one of them will ever see the land I promised on oath to their forefathers. No one who has treated me with contempt will ever see it. But because my servant Caleb had a different spirit and follows me wholeheartedly, I will bring him into the land he went to, and his descendants will inherit it" (Num. 14:22-24, NIV).

Forty years passed by. A new generation came along, filled with enthusiasm, they were led by two elderly men of enthusiasm, Joshua and Caleb. *Jonah most certainly knew Caleb's story.*

The people of Israel had conquered most of the land but here and there were some cities on the hilltops that were strongly defended with tall walls that couldn't be taken. One day, standing outside a town called Hebron, Caleb said:

> Now then, just as the Lord promised, he has kept me alive for forty-five years since the time he said this to Moses, while Israel moved about in the desert. So here I am today, eighty-five years old! I am still as strong today as the day Moses sent me out; I'm just as vigorous to go out to battle now as I was then. Now give me this hill country that the Lord promised me that day. You yourself heard then that the Anakites were there, and their cities were large and fortified, but, the Lord helping me, I will drive them out just as he said [Josh. 14:10-12, NIV].

Caleb's chief characteristic was that he wholly followed the Lord. And Jonah knew that story because he had read the Book of Joshua.

Jonah didn't know the story of Timothy in the New Testament, which expressed the same thoughts. Paul wrote to Timothy, "Be diligent in these matters; give yourself wholly to them, so that everyone may see your progress" (1 Tim. 4:15).

At the graduate school where I teach, someone asked recently, "Why is it that some ministers succeed and some fail?" The answer seems to be that some ministers give God and their calling their whole hearts and some do not. I have known many men who have been in the ministry. Some were highly talented, some were well educated, but after many years, those who remain are the ones who gave themselves wholly, completely, to the things of God. Some others equally or more talented have eventually dropped away because they did not.

The widow who gave the temple treasury the two mites, two copper coins, is not known by name, but her gift is unforgettable. Jesus stood with the disciples at the treasury and saw this woman and said, "They all gave out of their wealth; but she, out of her poverty, put in everything—all she had to live on" (Mark 12:44).

In the young Jerusalem church, Christians sold property, brought the money and gave it to the Apostles. Peter said it was perfectly all right for them to keep their money or give all of it. But Ananias and Sapphira came to the apostles and said they were giving all the money from the sale of their property, when as a matter of fact, they held part of it back. The Book of Acts tells that the Holy Spirit took their lives; not for giving half the money, not even for holding part of it back; but for claiming that they had given it all, when in fact they had given only a portion. Peter said to them, "You have not lied to men but to God" (See Acts 5:1-11, NIV).

What a contrast there is in these two stories! Here was a widow who did not have very much, yet dependent upon it as she was, she gave it all. Ananias and Sapphira gave far more than the widow, yet because they weren't wholehearted, but lied, they became the New Testament's first object lesson of judgment.

Giving God less than his best was another of Jonah's sins. It could be ours!

NINE

Tempted to Run Away from God
(Sin Number Five)

Most Christians know the hymn "I'll go where you want me to go, dear Lord; I'll say what you want me to say." Another version of this poem that would be good for us to keep in mind would be, "I'll go where you want me to go, dear Lord; I'll *stay* where you want me to *stay*." That would indeed be the song of a completely yielded life.

What a tragedy that the prophet Jonah could not have said that! The attitude it conveys would have spared him much trouble and would have blessed his life and ministry.

Our sins are illuminated when we see

the sins committed by the characters of the
Bible, which is one reason why we have the
historical portion of the Scriptures. The
Bible itself says, "These things happened to
them as examples and were written down
as warnings for us, on whom the fulfill-
ment of the ages has come" (1 Cor. 10:11,
NIV).

That is why we are told such shocking
stories as David's great sin, Moses's tendency
to lose his temper, the irritability and
emotional instability of the prophet Elijah,
"a man subject to like passions as we are"
(James 5:17).

We are told of the impulsiveness of
Peter, of the intolerant spirit of James and
John who are called, "the sons of thunder."
On one occasion these two asked Jesus
about a little village where the people had
refused to hear them. "Lord, do you want us
to call down fire from heaven to destroy
them?" (Luke 9:54, NIV). Jesus sorrowfully
and patiently rebuked them.

We are examining the sins of Jonah, not
that we may criticize a prophet long dead,
but that we may look at him and learn, for
we can see ourselves in him.

When Jonah was but a child, the
Assyrians had come into his country and
destroyed whole sections of it. Undoubtedly,
all his life Jonah had been brought up

hearing of their atrocities, and words of hate. He himself had come to hate the Ninevites.

Now a grown man, Jonah was a talented man, the court prophet. Of all the prophets of the northern part of Israel, he alone had been accepted into the presence of the king. In an age when most people could not read or write, Jonah was literate. Jonah was also a patriot, which is one reason why he did not want to respond when God commanded, "Arise, go to Nineveh, that great city, and cry against it; for their wickedness is come up before me" (1:2). He certainly didn't want to give them a chance to repent. He must have wanted them punished.

Jonah was also a servant of God. We know because he delivered unto the king and unto the people messages from God. Had he not been God's servant, God would not have commissioned him to speak in his name. Authentic prophecies came from God through Jonah, so he was a real servant of God.

Jonah never doubted God's existence, however much trouble his own sin and emotional excesses brought him. He never once departed from the Lord in terms of his firm belief in God. Even when he was angrily and stubbornly running away from God, he never once doubted God's existence. He stiffened his neck though he would not bow his head.

But with all of these marvelous personal attributes, Jonah was nevertheless an unyielded man. He was unwilling to obey God. When he himself was faced with the decision, he gave in to his own feelings and ran away.

The Bible says that Jonah "was fleeing from the presence of the Lord." In a liberal seminary which I attended, a professor said, "The Hebrews did not believe at first that God was universal—he was simply their god. The Assyrians had their god, and Egyptians had theirs. Yahweh was not considered to be the God of the entire Holy Land. He was only the God of the mountains of Judea and Samaria while the plains were not considered under Yahweh's jurisdiction." I recall that the professor, who is now dead and knows better, said, "Jonah thought that he could get beyond Yahweh's jurisdiction." This was not true, for Jonah himself said to the sailors, "I fear the Lord, the God of heaven, which hath made the sea and the dry land" (1:9). In Jonah's mind, he was only trying to run from the presence and fellowship of God. But he wasn't running away from the jurisdiction of God. He realized it for he confessed to the sailors, "I know that for my sake this great tempest is upon you" (1:12).

The point is that God was never considered by the Hebrews to be merely the God of the hills of Judea and Samaria, but was known as the King over all the earth. The Psalmist could later write, "Where can I go from your Spirit? Where can I flee from your presence? If I go to the heavens, you are there. If I make my bed in the depths, you are there" (Ps. 139:7, 8, NIV).

The Hebrews recognized that Yahweh was the one true God of all the earth and that there is no such possibility as running away from God's will.

We are all sometimes tempted to run away from God-given responsibilities. Psychologists tell us that there is the desire in everyone to return sometimes to the safety and the security of the womb. Subconsciously, we want to return to the time when there was complete security, where no decisions needed to be made, when we were safe, comfortable, and unchallenged. Birth is a traumatic experience and ever afterwards some people resent having been born. You have heard people say, "I wish I had never been born."

During my teen years, like other young people, I would use the argument with my parents, "I didn't ask to be born," one of the silliest arguments that has ever been used. But it comforted me then because, in a sense, I was really trying to run away from discipline, trouble, or blame.

We all feel, as the old proverb has it, "The grass is greener on the other side of the fence." We suppose today's troubles would diminish if we could just change our environment.

Jonah could not emotionally bear to preach God's message of judgment and possible repentance to Ninevites, for he hated the Assyrians. It is just as you and I could not have gone to Hitler during World War II and cheerfully preached forgiveness to him.

We could multiply this illustration as widely as we wish—we can at least understand Jonah's feelings. If our relatives had been killed, our land laid waste, and if those fierce, implacable, hostile and sadistic Assyrian butchers had invaded our land, would we readily have forgiven them?

Like Jonah, we all want to run from difficult things. We are all frustrated. We all take on more burdens at times than we have any business trying to bear. We all have unpleasantness facing us, we all become fed up with other people. We all share the same humanity. We are all sinners,

and consequently, at times we want to run
from whatever God tells us to do.

But when Jonah ran from God, it meant
for him to forsake God's very purpose for
his life. I've known many people who have
tried to run away from life, duty, promises,
difficulties and heavy burdens, when God
had told them to stay and obey him.

Being tempted to run from God's directives
may be a common human response, but it
always leads us outside the will of God.
God's will for us could be described as a
circle. As long as we stay within that
circle, his will is supreme in our lives. "All
things work together for good" is the
promise from God only as long as we stay
within his will. But if we deliberately run,
we can no longer claim the promise of
Romans 8:28.

At times, God must be terribly disappointed with us. He has spent much time
to train us. Every experience we have had
in life so far has been incorporated in God's
purpose for our lives. God can take
whatever comes our way, good or bad, and
he can weave it into his pattern as a fine
tapestry is woven. But we may forget that a
tapestry usually has dark threads as well as
light.

Sometimes when God wishes to use us

in some great and mighty way, that is the moment that Satan tempts us most to want to run away from God.

When Jonah reached Nineveh, he preached and the whole city, the capital of the greatest empire on earth at that time, repented. On the eve of this mission for which his whole life had been a preparation, which would go down in history as one of the great spiritual awakenings of all time, Jonah ran away!

Jonah surely rationalized his decision. A "reason" is the actual cause for which we do something. What we term "rationalization" is an attempt to convince ourselves and others that we are doing the right thing when deep down we know that we aren't. Rationalization gives us a socially acceptable excuse, something which sounds logical, that people will accept, but which only resembles the truth. We all rationalize at times. We are called to go to the places of God's destiny yet we look for every reason possible to run someplace else and then explain away our disobedience by some reasonable sounding excuse.

I am sure that Jonah must have said to himself, "There is a wonderful city in Spain. I can minister effectively in Tarshish." But Jonah had forgotten something. If he went to Nineveh, he went with God's authentic message. If he went to Tarshish, he could not speak in the name of the Lord because God wouldn't go with him. He could have talked about God, but he couldn't have spoken for God, which is a big difference.

Jonah placed his emotions at the top, his common sense at the bottom. Every time we want to run away from God, every time we are tempted to flee from his presence, we are usually putting our emotions first and listening to them instead of listening to reason. As Jonah got into trouble when he ran away from God, when we run from whatever God wants us to do, we will also get into trouble.

God's principles set forth in the story of Jonah are in such clear terms that none can miss them. The lesson is inescapable. Today, if we are running away from God, we badly need to heed his warning illustrated by Jonah's story.

What does God want us to do? First, he wants us to do his will. When Jonah was brought up out of the whale, he had to do exactly what God had told him to do in the first place. That whale trip was not really necessary, because when he came back to God, the same commandment was staring him in the face and he still had to go and do it.

Unfortunately, Jonah did not do so in the

right spirit. God wanted Jonah, and he
wants us, to say, "I delight to do thy will."

Is that asking too much? There are times
when we would almost rather do anything
other than God's will. In the end, however,
we are brought to it. Even then we may
say, "I'll do it, but I am not going to like it."

God wants us lovingly, joyfully to
embrace his will in faith. He wants us to
believe that what he tells us to do is the
best use to which we could put our lives.
God won't ask us to do something that is
harmful to us. Because he is good he wants
only that which is best for us and which
fulfills us best.

God invites us to Christ because he
wants to give us the most glorious and
power-filled life that we can possibly know.
We cannot enjoy life, have much zest, live
victoriously or as happily in any other way
than by the means he has provided. He
knows what is best.

The world seems attractive, but being
attractive is what the world is all about!
The world's style consists of making this
present life and the standards of our times
seem attractive. It has the money and the
system to do it. When we see this truth, we
realize that in contrast to the way of God,
this present world is fatally attractive.

Ultimately it is the way of death. A person who takes the time to look, can see the skull behind the painted grin.

God wants us to learn from Jonah to stop restlessly moving about. As it says in the New Testament, "Having done all, stand." We Californians are statistically a moving people. One of four of us will move next year. We are a restless, foot-loose people. Perhaps it is time that some of us begin to ask, "Does God use people best when they stay or when they keep on running about from place to place?"

The answer is plain from the story of Jonah. You have to live a long time or have shattering experiences to learn what happens to people who make wrong decisions. I have noticed that, in the ministry, the average preacher changes churches every three and one-third years. But usually the pastors that do the greatest work are those that stay in one church for decades.

I teach pastors at the California Graduate School of Theology and I tell them, "Find wherever God's will is, settle down, and stay there. Make your mistakes and when necessary, repent. You will play the fool sometimes because you are human, but when you do, ask the people to forgive you and stay and stay and stay." I don't know a truly effective ministry where there have been a great many pastoral changes in a man's life.

The ministry should ideally be one that lasts. One that lasts is one that stays and obeys. If that is true about the ministry, it is also true about our lives.

A recent television program was called "This Was Entertainment." It was about the great moments in some of the MGM films of yesteryear. One scene was of a great banquet held in 1955 where all the great stars of that time were present. They ran the camera down the tables and I saw people whose names were then familiar, not only in America but all over the world. Then I realized that today they are either very aged, or in many instances, dead. Most are already forgotten and yet the scene seemed as if it were filmed yesterday. But it wasn't. It was made twenty-five years ago! It reminded me that time is passing very quickly and every once in a while, we are suddenly made aware that in a few years our time for doing God's will will have run out.

How many years do we have left? Every time we have a funeral at our church, I say to myself, "What did that person think the last time he came to church? He didn't know that the ribbon of life was to be spun off the spool in a matter of hours or days." It is a solemn thought.

Since time is so short, we mustn't make any mistakes with it, or waste it. We must use it as if we are aware that we have a limited time. We certainly have only a little time in which to find and do God's will just as Jonah did.

TEN

Tempted to Question God's Wisdom
(Sin Number Six)

The prophet Jonah was sinful as we all are at times. Yet his sins were those of the spirit—not of the flesh. When the Phoenician sailors heard his confession that God had sent the storm on the sea because of his disobedience, they did not at first fully believe his story but rowed frantically to save the ship. Later they did agree to throw him overboard.

The person of the world defines sin far differently than does the Christian. To the worldling, sin is some shocking behavior, such as a crime or an act against society or decency. But Jesus said that the inner thoughts which arise from within us are the sources of sin and defilement.

Jonah's sin was that he had a defiant spirit. This prophet who was supposed to be an authentic voice from God at that time, found himself yielding to the temptation of questioning God's message, disagreeing with God's judgment. Imagine the audacity of a mere man, and God's prophet at that, disputing God's wisdom!

POSSIBLE RATIONALIZATIONS

One can imagine that Jonah could have questioned whether or not the voice he heard was the authentic voice of God. But God had spoken and Jonah knew it. He just didn't want to obey God.

Jonah could have supposed that God's commandment to preach God's judgment on Nineveh was the product of his imagination. But the test of the Book of Jonah reveals no evidence that he doubted that the voice he heard was actually that of God.

The historic record is clear. Jonah simply disagreed with God. A careful reading shows that whatever else Jonah was, he was honest and willing to forfeit his life rather than agree with God.

Jonah did not alibi even to the sailors.

He frankly named his sin. Nor would he give it up until he was three days and three nights in the terrifying grave of the whale's stomach.

The most astonishing aspect of Jonah's sin was that he and God wanted the same thing in the end. This is frequently true with God and us today.

WHAT JONAH WANTED

Jonah wanted no mercy for the merciless Ninevites. The ravagers of his country were, to Jonah's thinking, beyond the compassion of God. He was not only a patriot, he was a partisan. If he had believed that God would actually pour out the wrath of divine justice upon Nineveh, it seems from the account that Jonah would have been only too glad to preach that bad news to the despised Assyrians.

It was the fear that the bad news might turn to good news that hardened Jonah's heart. He chided God, "I knew that thou art a gracious God, and merciful, slow to anger, and of great kindness, and repentest thee of the evil" (4:2).

Had Jonah been praying instead of rebelling, he might have thought ahead. In the end, what he really wanted was freedom for Israel from future Assyrian oppression. And there was nothing amiss with that, but he sought it in the wrong way.

WHAT GOD WANTED

Jonah would have been mightily surprised to have learned that much of what he really desired, though he tried to get it through improper means, was also what God was seeking. For God knew that if Nineveh repented of its violence, there would be no more invasions of Israel for generations to come.

That result was, of course, what eventually came to pass. The wave of repentance which swept Nineveh, from king to commoner, apparently wiped out Assyrian oppression for the next sixty years. Not until the time of a later king, Tiglath-Pileser, do we find a record of another Assyrian invasion of Israel, and that was three generations after Jonah's time. Then ten years after that, Israel was taken captive of Assyria in 721 B.C. by Shalmaneser.

But in Jonah's day, God proposed the way to accomplish what Jonah and Israel so deeply desired: no more war and no more threats of invasion. God's way was to extend to the city of Nineveh his mercy, based upon Assyria's repentance. God's way was better than Jonah's way. Yet Jonah's shortsightedness and his distrust of God's wisdom might conceivably have prevented Israel's freedom from being finally secured for generations.

God could have done his will with Assyria despite Jonah. But it is obvious that God does not often choose to override the human instruments he has chosen. Otherwise, Satan would long ago have been in the bottomless pit and there would be no temptation, no sin, and no death.

God could have raised up someone other than Jonah to bring revival to Nineveh, but then we would never have learned from this famous story the value of trusting God's wisdom rather than our own opinions.

WHAT WE WANT

Our personal desires may not resemble those of Jonah's in appearance. But, when we think of it we, like Jonah, usually seek whatever "happiness" may mean to us. Our "Assyrians" may not impale people on stakes. Our problems may not be related to racial pride, racial hatred, vainglorious nationalism or to fury with others. But any rebellious desire is only superficially unlike others.

When our quest for happiness runs counter to the revealed will of God, we may often suppose that God does not want our happiness. Too frequently young people face some social conflict with the will of God and then, like Jonah, rise up to flee from the presence of the Lord to some "Tarshish." But God has never been the enemy of happiness, which is fleeting. In fact, he wishes to give us something better than happiness, and that is joy. Joy lasts. It is good in fair weather and foul.

Like Jonah, we often suppose happiness lies in following our instincts or prejudices. But if we think so, we are wrong. Joy comes even more abundantly than we can imagine when we follow the will of God.

Unlike Jonah, we should take the long look. Demas was one of Paul's followers, of whom the Apostle wrote, "Demas hath forsaken me, having loved this present world" (2 Tim. 4:10).

Like Paul, Demas is long dead, but Demas probably died without faith or honor. Paul, had he chosen to do so, could have made a higher mark and enjoyed greater honor in "this present world" than Demas ever could. But Paul was right in turning away from the world, choosing instead the will of God and the joy of surrender. Demas was terribly wrong in rejecting the will of God. This is history's final harsh verdict.

Or consider Moses who could have inherited the throne of Egypt, but who chose rather "to suffer affliction with the people of God, than to enjoy the pleasures of sin for a season; esteeming the reproach of Christ greater riches than the treasures in Egypt" (Heb. 11:25, 26).

Jonah failed to see that refusing to share God's grace with his enemies could later have meant doom to his own people. His God-directed message to Assyria was not only about their need for repentance, but also, God's way of deliverance for Israel. God's ways are not our ways, but are higher than the heavens compared to our ways and thoughts.

ELEVEN

Tempted to Forget the Power of God
(Sin Number Seven)

There is much to learn about God's power in the lives of the prophets of ancient Israel. They were men of obedient faith who frequently experienced two results of their calling.

First, they were given the power from God to see the future and speak to people about it. Moses testified to this type of man when he quoted God as promising: "I will raise them up a Prophet from among their brethren, like unto thee, and will put my words in his mouth; and he shall speak unto them all that I shall command him" (Deut. 18:18).

Second, these prophets were given divine

power to work miracles. So the Book of Jonah is, among other things, a book about the power of God as manifested in both message and miracle.

This miraculous power of God is clearly evident in every episode in the Book of Jonah. Note the supernatural evidences of God at work.

God gave a message, a divine directive, to Jonah for delivery to Nineveh. God sent out a stormy wind to stop Jonah from fleeing by sea. After Jonah was thrown overboard, God calmed the raging seas. God prepared a fish to swallow Jonah. God caused Jonah to stay alive inside the fish. God caused the fish to vomit Jonah out near the shore. God gave his message to Jonah a second time. Jonah delivered God's message to Nineveh and the people there "believed God" and the greatest revival in known history ensued. God prepared a gourd vine to cover Jonah. God prepared a worm to destory the vine. God sent an east wind to remind Jonah. All of these acts of God were miraculous.

Since Jonah was an accredited prophet who predicted the future by the message of God to King Jeroboam II (2 Kings 14:25) we are certain that at one time he really knew and experienced the anointing of God's power.

As recorded in the Book of Jonah,

miracles of God were clearly evident on these eleven occasions mentioned above. Yet, the story of Jonah is that of a man who ignored, overlooked, or neglected the very power of God which he had known and upon which he, as a prophet, should have depended.

HOW JONAH'S EXPERIENCE SPEAKS TO US TODAY

Jonah's experience speaks to us about the fact that no matter how often we see the evidence of God's power clearly displayed, if our hearts are not right, we will not respond to God's will but become hardened in stubborn rebellion. For example, people can see God's power in a church service and still remain unmoved themselves. Jonah was like this.

Christians can have experienced God's power in the past but if their hearts are not right, they can still run away from God's will in the present. One would think that eleven miraculous events would have awed Jonah into glad obedience, but they did not.

The Book of Jonah speaks to us about the reasons the prophet's heart was not right—a state so terrible that even repeated evidences of God's power could not persuade him to fulfill his calling. Jonah entertained four evils in his heart. He was disobedient and wanted to run away from God; he was filled with a deep anger at God; he was stubborn and unyielding; and he was given to self-pity though God's will was plain to him.

If we too entertain these evils, the power of God may have to be taken from us and turned against us, as was the case with Jonah. Thus Paul warned the misbehaving Corinthians: "But when we are judged, we are chastened of the Lord, that we should not be condemned with the world" (1 Cor. 11:32).

CONCLUSION

The Book of Jonah speaks to us about the tragic waste which always comes from failing God. Had Jonah experienced obedient faith, he could have been the instrument of God's power from the beginning. A whole section of his life is a blank, a loss.

Had Jonah experienced obedient faith, he could have avoided much personal trouble and miserable suffering. As the old hymn reminds us: "Oh, what peace we often forfeit; Oh, what needless pain we bear."

God wished for revival—Jonah wished for death. Had Jonah gained his wish for death, which he mentioned five times, he would have never been further used of God on earth. Instead, he would have entered eternity as a failure, without the reward of enlarged capacity for service.

But God's patience is long. Jonah at least learned his lesson. Not sparing or excusing his sins, he left us a record which was later incorporated into the Book of Jonah. It is both a testimony and a warning.

We have reason to believe that his faith was restored as his willingness to embrace God's will returned. Jonah was, indeed, a sinner, but the story of his sins is part of the prophetic word, written as an example for us upon whom the end of the age is coming.